E S T A T E   P U B L I C

LONDON BOROUGH OF BROM

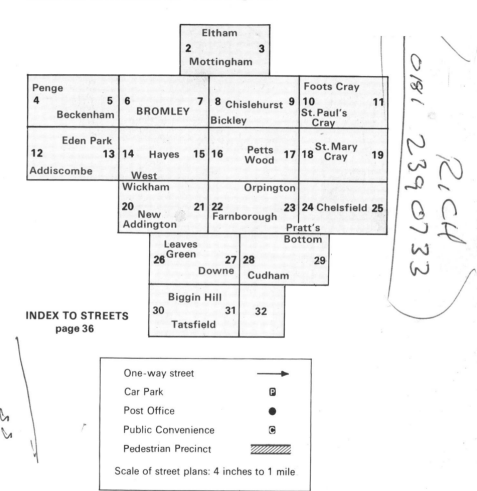

	Eltham		
	2	3	
		Mottingham	

Penge					Foots Cray	
4	5	6	7	8 Chislehurst 9	10	11
Beckenham		BROMLEY		Bickley	St. Paul's Cray	

Eden Park
12   13 | 14   Hayes   15 | 16   Petts Wood 17 | 18 St. Mary Cray 19
Addiscombe

West Wickham
20   New Addington   21 | 22   Farnborough   23 | 24 Chelsfield 25

Orpington

Pratt's Bottom

Leaves Green
26   27 | 28   29
Downe   Cudham

Biggin Hill
30   31 | 32
Tatsfield

INDEX TO STREETS
page 36

One-way street	→
Car Park	P
Post Office	●
Public Convenience	C
Pedestrian Precinct	▨

Scale of street plans: 4 inches to 1 mile

Street plans prepared and published by ESTATE PUBLICATIONS, Bridewell House, Tenterden, Kent and based upon the ORDNANCE SURVEY maps with the sanction of the controller of H.M. Stationery Office.

The publishers acknowledge the co-operation of the London Borough of Bromley in the preparation of these maps.

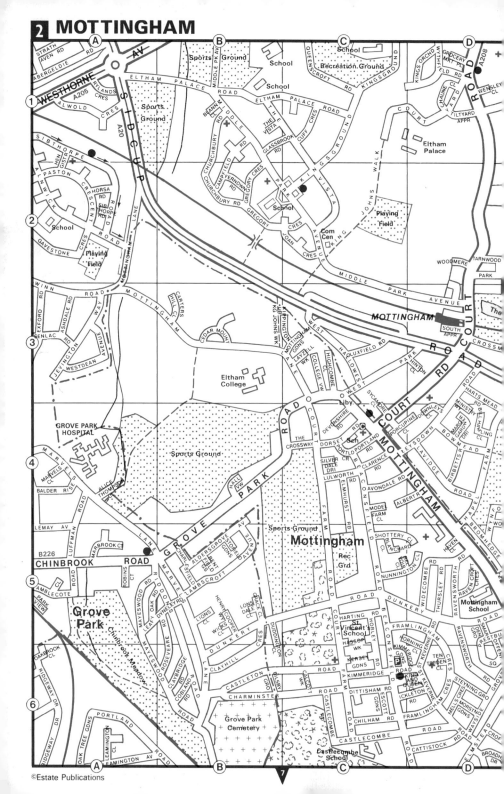

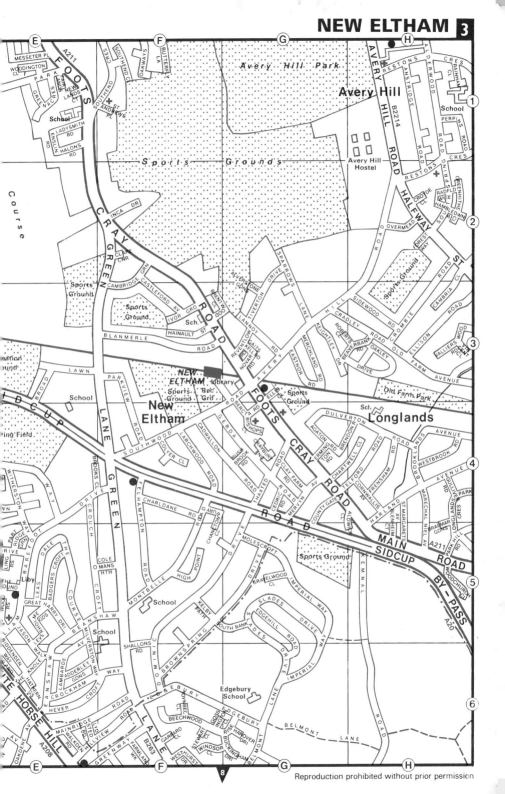

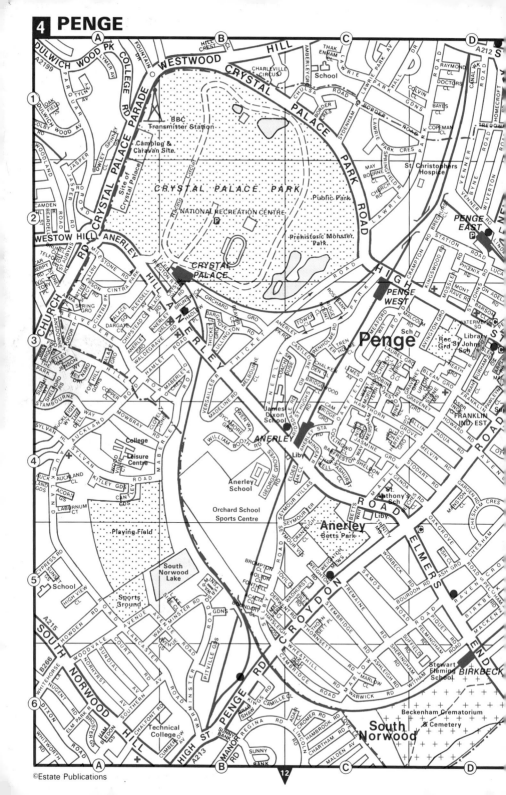

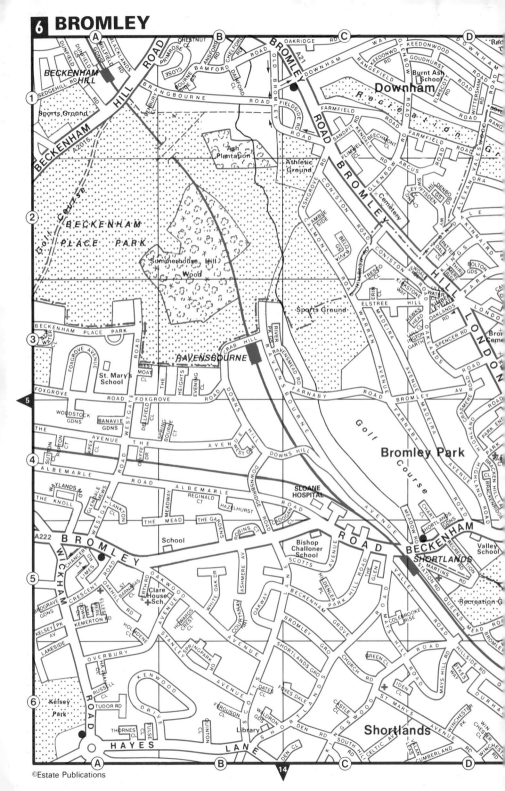

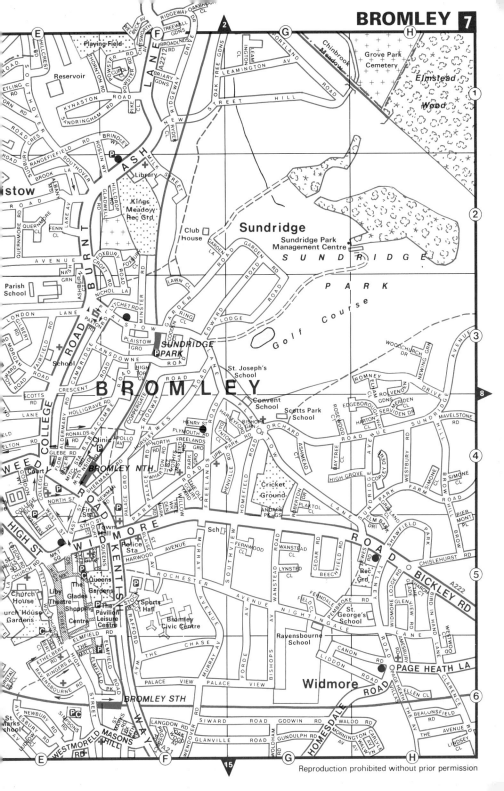

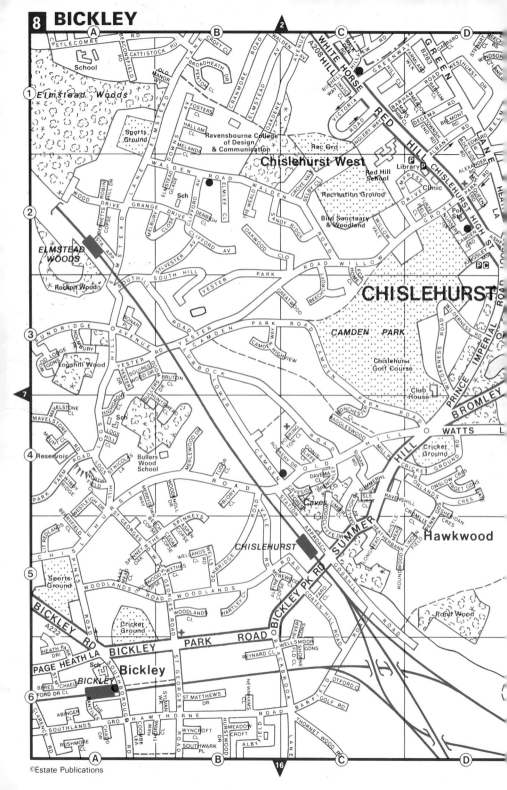

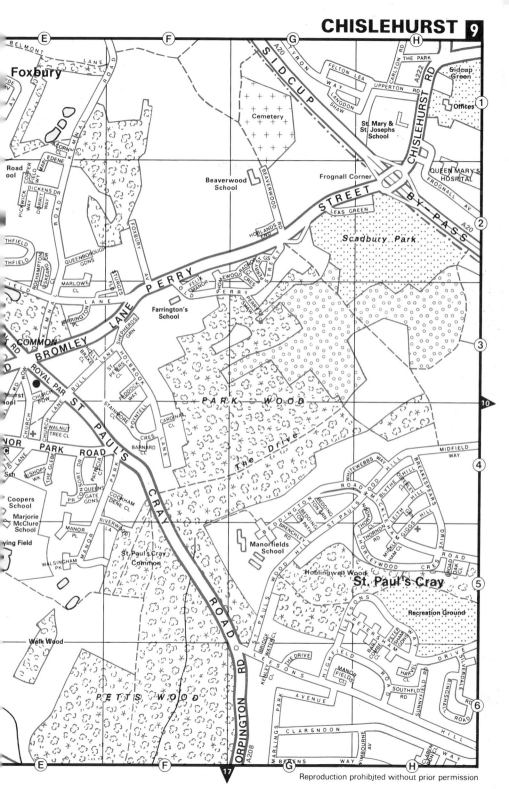

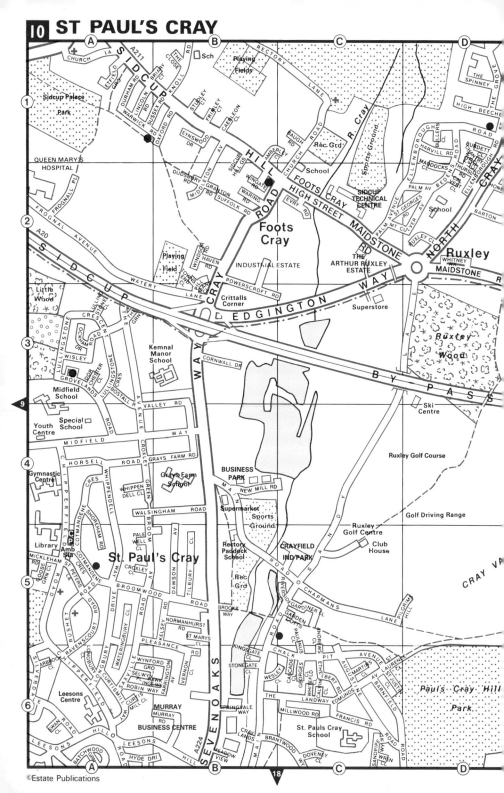

©Estate Publications

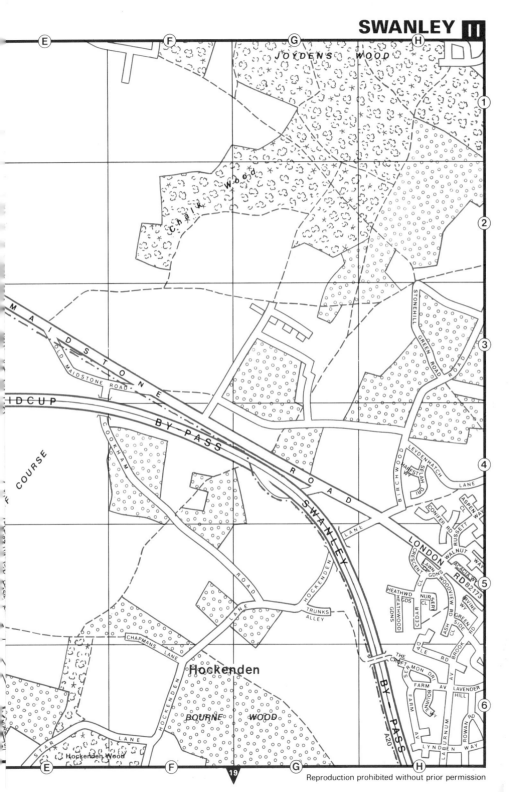

SWANLEY

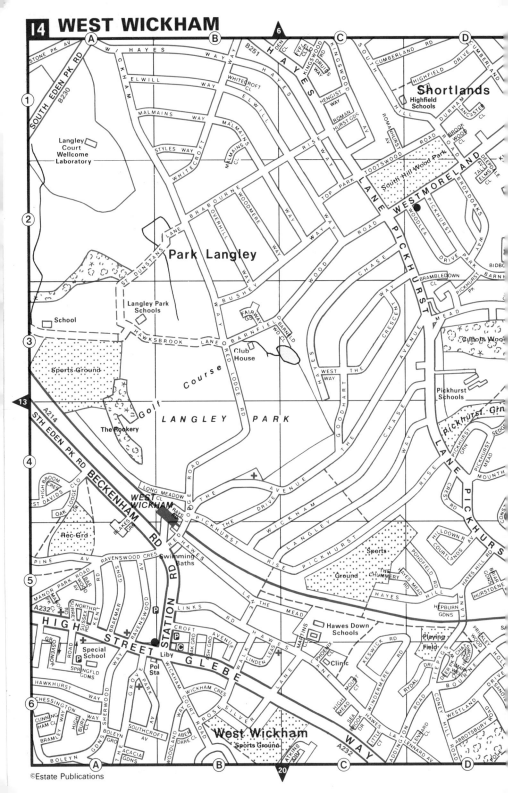

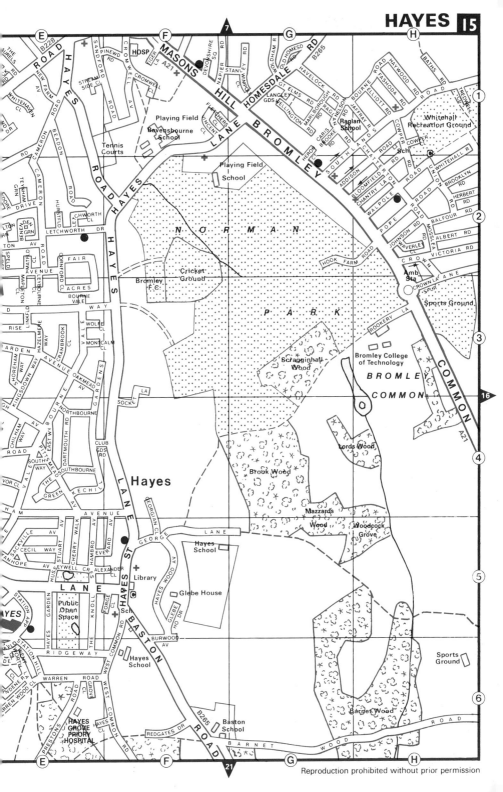

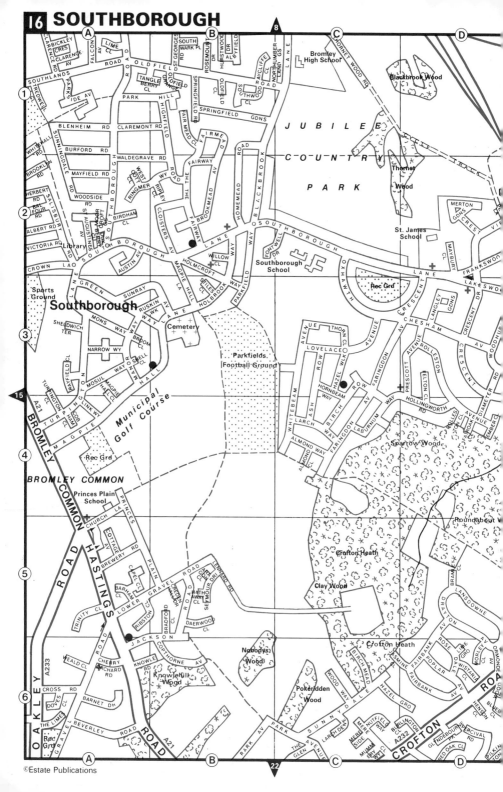

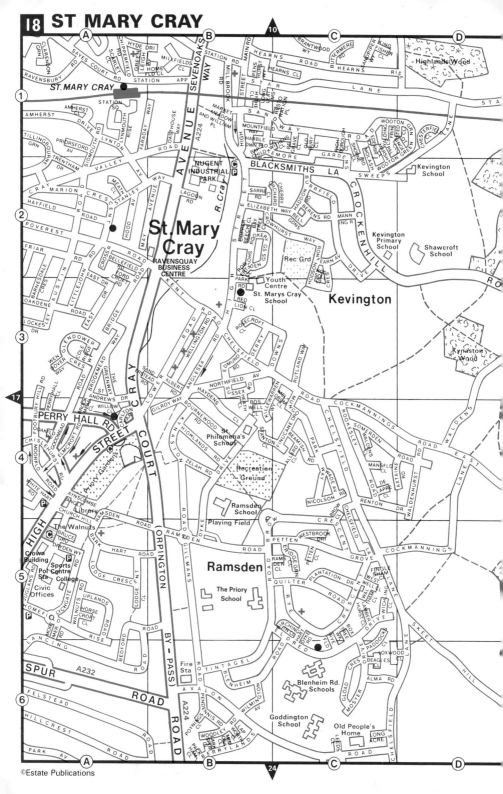

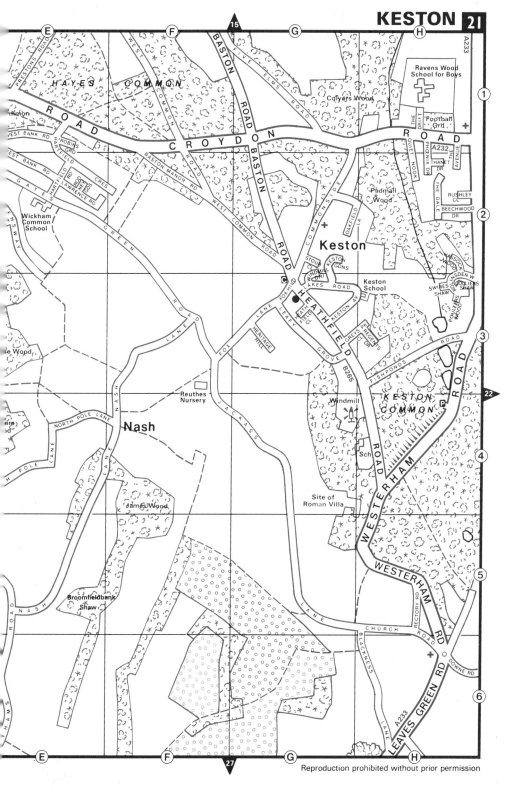

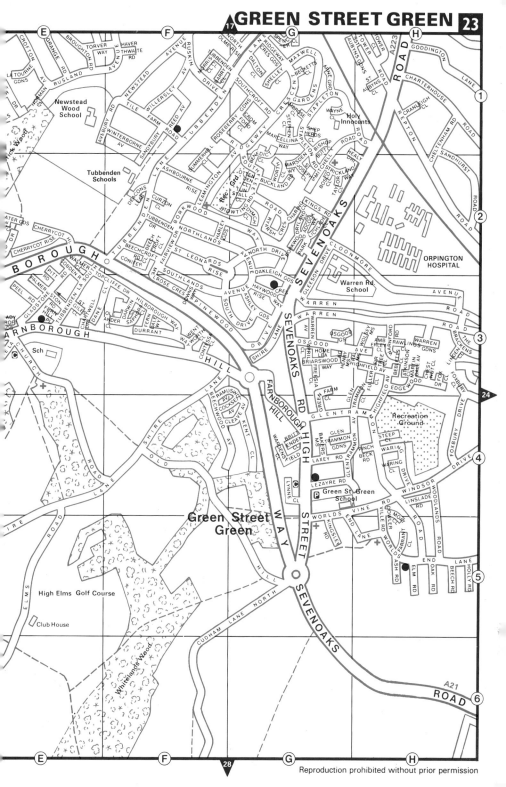

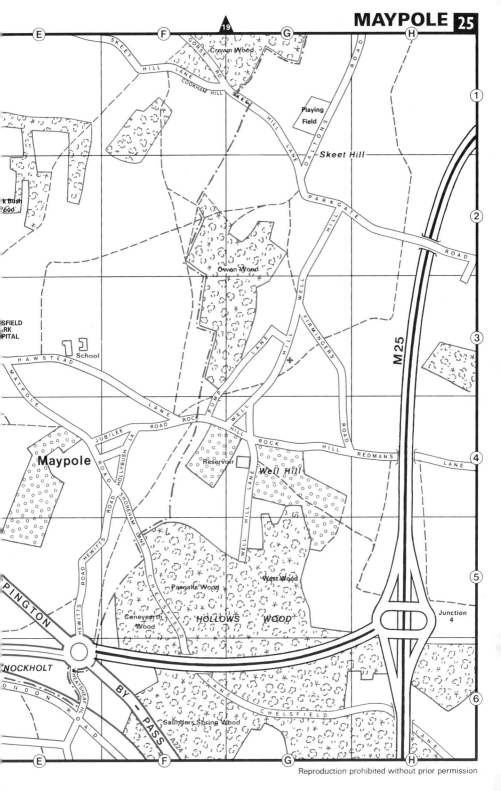

19

E F G H

Crown Wood

SKEET HILL LANE
GORSE RD
COOKHAM HILL
SKEET HILL LANE

1

Playing Field

DALTONS ROAD

Skeet Hill

2

PARKGATE
HILL

ROAD

k Bush ood

WELL

FIRMINGERS

M25

Owen Wood

+

3

SFIELD RK PITAL

HAWSTEAD

School

LANE

HILL

Maypole
MAYPOLE ROAD

JUBILEE ROAD ROCK

HOLLYBUSH LA

PUMP HILL
WELL HILL

ROCK HILL

REDMANS LANE

4

Reservoir

Well Hill

HEWITTS ROAD
SHOREHAM LANE
CHELSFIELD

ROAD HILL

West Wood

Paggalls Wood

5

HOLLOWS WOOD

Coneyearth Wood

PINGTON

Junction 4

NOCKHOLT

BY - PASS

WHEATSHEAF HILL

CHELSFIELD LANE

6

ONDON RD

A224

Saunders Spring Wood

CHELSFIELD LANE

21

A B C D

1

ARAGON CL
YARBANK CRES
Sports
Ground

2

KING

HOMES
MEAD WM
HENRYS
FAIR
CHILDES
AV

West Wickham
Reservoir

3

Schools

Playing Field

LAYHAMS

Hopperhatch Wood

Furze Bottom

ASHMORE

MOUCHOTTE
CLOSE
HENDERSON RD
TURNER RD
WHITTIMER

SHEEPBARN   LANE

HIGHAMS HILL

Jewels Wood

JEWELS HILL

KEN PK CRES
GRICE AV
HANBURY DR
VINCENT CLOS

4

ROAD

SALTBOX
OAKLANDS

MAIN

5

PAR
BLACKMANS LA

HILL

OAKLANDS

M

6

CROWN

ASH   LANE

LANE

VICTORIA
GS

A B C D

30

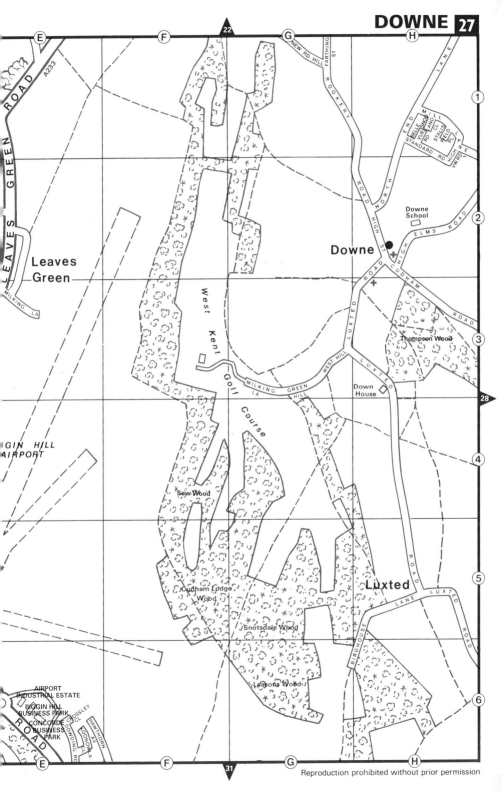

Leaves Green

GREEN ROAD

A233

LEAVES

MILKING LA

New Rd Hill

Farthing St

ROOKERY

HIGH ROAD

NORTH

Downe School

Downe

West Kent

Golf Course

MILKING LA

GREEN HILL

WEST HILL

LUXTED ROAD

LUXTED

Down House

Thompson Wood

CUDHAM ROAD

ELMS ROAD

HIGH ST

GIN HILL
AIRPORT

Sew Wood

Cudham Lodge Wood

Snotsdale Wood

Luxted

LUXTED ROAD

BIRDHOUSE LANE

Leasons Wood

AIRPORT INDUSTRIAL ESTATE

BIGGIN HILL BUSINESS PARK

CONCORDE BUSINESS PARK

CROSSLEY CL

HAWTHORN

DOWDING RD

KONONA

ROAD

END MILL

BELLE VUE RD

STATION RD

VW RD

STANDARD RD

HIGH RD

FIELD CL

LANE

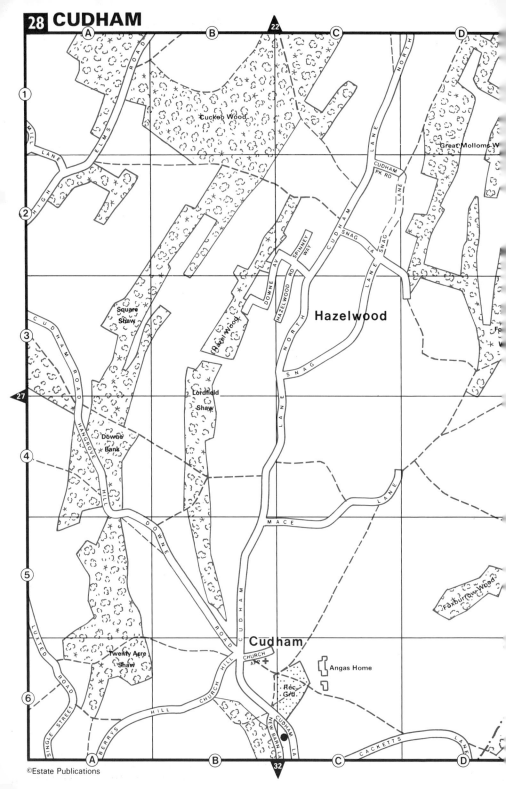

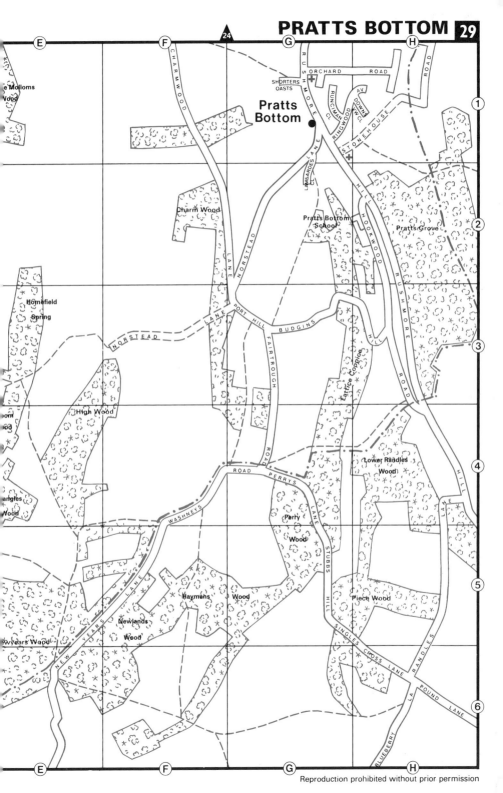

Pratts Bottom

SHORTERS OASTS

ORCHARD ROAD

CHARMWOOD

RUSHMORE

RUNCIMAN ROAD

RINGWOOD

DOWNS AV.

STONEHOUSE ROAD

LAMBARDES LANE

Charm Wood

Pratts Bottom School

Pratts Grove

HOOKWOOD

HILL

NORSTEAD LANE

PORT HILL

FAIRTROUGH

BUDGINS

Homefield Spring

NORSTEAD LANE

High Wood

Lattice Coppice

RUSHMORE ROAD

ROAD

Lower Randles Wood

ROAD

PERRYS LANE

Parry Wood

WASHNEYS LANE

HILL LANE

angles Wood

STUBBS HILL

Haymans Wood

Piece Wood

NEW YEARS LANE

Newlands Wood

wyears Wood

SINGLES CROSS LANE

RANDLES LANE

LA POUND LANE

BLUEBERRY

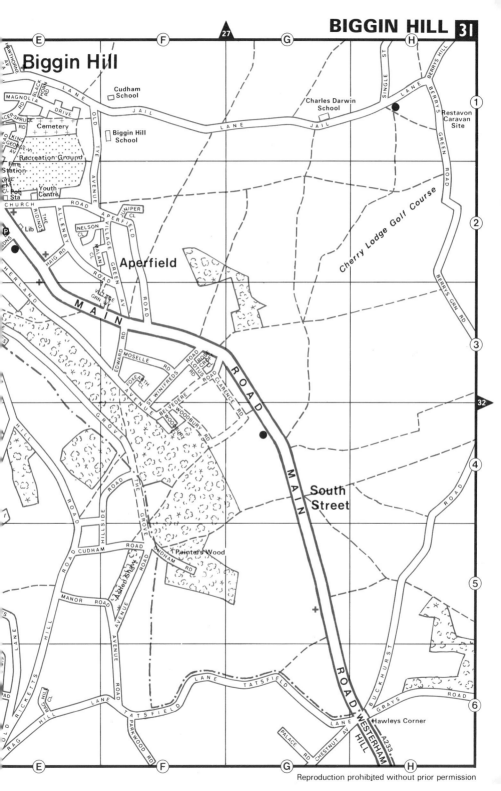

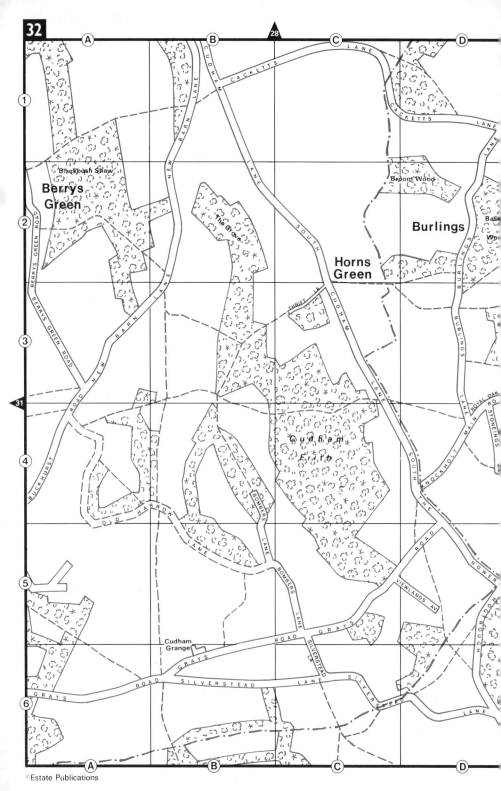

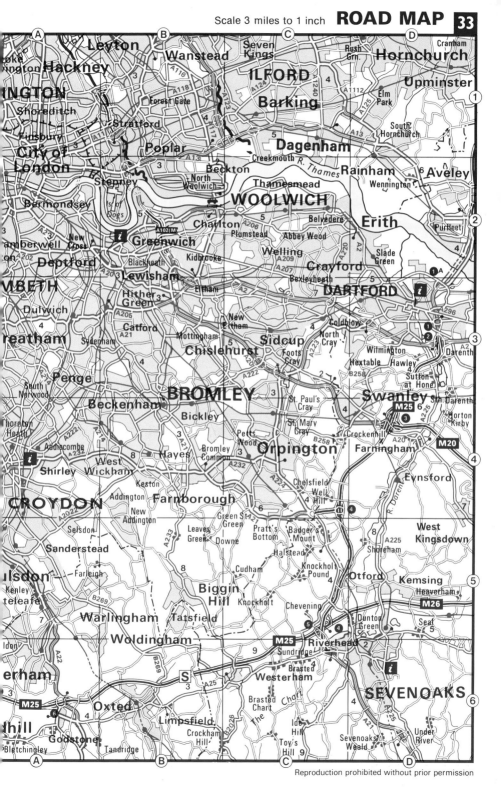

LONDON BOROUGH OF BROMLEY

Bromley Borough is an area of contrasts with rolling green fields and wooded hills in the south-east and built up areas in the north and west. Although within easy reach of central London the region has strong identity. Bromley, Beckenham, Orpington, Penge and Chislehurst are the major towns which give the area its own special character.

It is also the largest of the London Boroughs covering around 59 square miles. The Borough lies in the south-east corner of Greater London, extending from Crystal Palace in the north-west to the border of Swanley in the east and Biggin Hill in the south.

It is predominantly residential and has small belts of light industry, modern business premises and up-to-date shopping thoroughfares.

There are good facilities for all branches of sport with swimming pools and leisure centres at Bromley, West Wickham, Beckenham and Orpington. Crystal Palace has the National Sports Centre which caters for participants and spectators. There is an athletics track at Norman Park and numerous golf courses throughout the Borough. A range of parks and nature reserves offer a selection of interesting walks.

Over 1,500 organisations, clubs and societies exist in the area together with a comprehensive adult education service which allows residents to pursue a wide range of interests.

Regular train and bus services connect all parts of the Borough with the City and West End as well as providing vital links within the region.

For further details please ring the Civic Centre on 081-464 3333.

N.B. — This map has been carefully prepared and brought up-to-date at the time of going to press. However, ongoing development in the Borough means that work completed shortly after publication of this map will not be included. Queries concerning locations should be addressed to the Bromley Civic Centre, Stockwell Close, Bromley BR1 3UH.

CAR PARKS — PUBLIC

Location	Capacity
BECKENHAM	
*St. George's Road, Beckenham	153
Fairfield Road, Beckenham	105
Village Way, Beckenham (Multi-storey)	283
Lennard Road, Beckenham	45
Dunbar Avenue, Elmers End	67
Cannon Cinema, Beckenham	55
Penge East	70
CHISLEHURST	
Red Hill, Chislehurst	38
High Street, Chislehurst	142
*Cotmandine Crescent, St. Paul's Cray	38
Hornbrook House, High Street, Chislehurst	75
WEST WICKHAM	
Station Road, West Wickham	76
High Street, West Wickham	138
Ravenswood Avenue, West Wickham	170
Coney Hall	26

Location	Capacity
BROMLEY	
The Hill, Beckenham Lane (Multi-storey)	70
Station Approach, Hayes	14
Station Road (except Thursday)	7
Westmoreland Road (Multi-storey)	59
Burnt Ash Lane	10
Plaistow Lane	7
Civic Centre (Multi-storey)	72
South Street (Saturday only)	5
Palace Grove (Saturday only)	8
Tweedy Road (temporary)	6
Masons Hill (temporary)	15
ORPINGTON	
67 Memorial Hall, Petts Wood	5
Station Road, Orpington (Multi-storey)	58
Queensway, Petts Wood	2
Lebanon Gardens, Biggin Hill	2
College of Further Education (Saturday only)	5
Homefield Rise	2

*Parking facilities available for commercial vehicles and coaches.

COUNCIL DEPARTMENTS

OUR MAIN SERVICES — WHO TO CONTACT

Bromley Civic Centre, Stockwell Close, Bromley BR1 3UH   081-464 3333

Borough Secretary

Legal work
Council and Committee
  agendas and other
  records
Electoral Services
Central telephones
Enquiries
Police liaison/Community
  Safety

Borough Treasurer

Council Tax
Business Rates
Housing Benefits

Chief Executive

Central personnel matters
Health and Safety
General Council
  management issues

Chief Engineer

Refuse collection
Roads
Sewers
Car parking
Public toilets
Council building
  maintenance
Traffic
Environmental strategy
Recycling
Street cleaning

Chief Planner

Planning applications
Building control
Local Land Charges
Tree preservation
Town and countryside
  improvements and
  conservation
Architecture and Quantity
  Surveying
Promotion and Design

Director of Education

Schools
Careers Service
Youth Service
Student awards
Adult Education

Director of Land and General Services

Trading Standards
Registration of Births,
  Deaths and Marriages
Land and Valuation
  Services
Biggin Hill Airport
Noise nuisance
Pest Control
Consumer advice
Food safety
Weights and Measures
Renovation grants
Entertainment licences
Pollution control

Director of Social Services and Housing

Social Services for
  children, families,
  elderly people and
  people with disabilities
Personal Care
Foster Care
Meals Service
Bus passes
Inspection & Registration
Residential care
Homeless families
Social Work
Occupational Therapy
Day Centres

Director of Leisure Services

Central Library
High Street
Bromley BR1 1EX

Tel: 081-460 9966

Parks and Open Spaces
Leisure Centres
Sports facilities
Libraries
Museum Service

Allotments
Cemeteries
Civic Halls
Arts
Ecology/Nature Centres

Please note that some services are not based at the same address as the Chief Officer

GETTING IT RIGHT
At Bromley Council
What to do if things go wrong?

Get in touch with the Department concerned; either call in, send a letter, or give us a ring.

Details of our services and our main addresses and 'phone numbers are listed on the back of this leaflet.

If you are not sure who to talk to, ring 081-464 3333 or ask at any enquiry desk. Explain the problem and they will help you to contact the right person.

LONDON BOROUGH OF BROMLEY
INDEX TO STREETS

Abbey La	5 H3
Abbey Park Estate	5 H3
Abbots Clo	17 E5
Abbots Way	13 E2
Abbotsbury Rd	14 D6
Aberdare Rd	14 B6
Abingdon Way	24 A2
Abinger Clo	8 A6
Acacia Clo, Penge	4 B5
Acacia Clo, Petts Wood	17 F2
Acacia Gdns	14 A6
Acacia Rd	5 F6
Acer Rd	31 E1
Acorn Clo	9 E1
Acorn Way	22 D2
Adams Rd	13 F2
Adcock Walk	23 G2
Addington Rd, Addington	20 A2
Addington Rd, West Wickham	14 C6
Addison Clo	17 E3
Addison Rd	15 G2
Adelaide Ct	5 G3
Adelaide Rd	8 D1
Ainsdale Clo	17 F5
Albany Mews	7 E2
Albany Rd	8 D1
Albemarle Park	5 H4
Albemarle Rd	6 A4
Albert Rd, Bromley	16 A2
Albert Rd, Chelsfield	24 A3
Albert Rd, St Mary Cray	18 B3
Albert Rd, SE 20	5 E2
Albert Rd, SE 9	2 D4
Albyfield	8 B6
Aldermary Rd	7 E4
Aldersmead Rd	5 F3
Alexander Clo	15 E5
Alexander Rd	8 D2
Alexandra Cres	6 D2
Alexandra Rd, Biggin Hill	30 C4
Alexandra Rd, SE 26	5 E2
Allandale Pl	24 D1
Allard Clo	18 C4
Allen Rd	5 E5
Allenby Rd	31 E2
Allington Rd	17 F6
Alma Pl	4 A3
Alma Rd	18 C6
Almond Clo	16 C4
Almond Way	16 C4
Alpine Copse	8 B5
Alton Gdns	5 G3
Altyre Clo	13 F2
Altyre Way	13 F2
Amberley Clo	23 H3
Ambleside Av	13 F2
Ambrose Clo	23 G1
Amesbury Rd	7 H6
Amhurst Clo	18 A1
Amhurst Dri	17 G1
Ancaster Mews	5 E6
Ancaster Rd	5 E6
Andace Park Gdns	7 G4
Andover Rd	17 F6
Andrews Clo	10 C5
Anerley Gro	4 A3
Anerley Hill	4 A2
Anerley Park	4 B3
Anerley Park Rd	4 B3
Anerley Rd	4 B3
Anerley Station Rd	4 C4
Anerley Vale	4 B3
Anglesea Rd	18 B3
Aperfield Rd	31 F2
Apex Clo	6 A4
Apollo Av	7 F4
Appledore Clo	15 E2
April Clo	23 G3
Arbor Clo	5 H5
Arbrook Clo	10 A6
Archer Rd	17 H2
Arden Gro	22 D2
Arne Gro	23 G1
Arpley Rd	4 D3
Arragon Gdns	20 A1
Arrol Rd	4 D6
Arthur Rd	30 D1
Artington Clo	23 E2
Arundel Dri	24 B3
Ascot Rd	17 G1
Ash Clo, Petts Wood	17 E2
Ash Clo, SE 20	4 D5
Ash Gro, SE 20	4 D5
Ash Gro, West Wickham	14 B6
Ash Rd	23 H5
Ash Row	16 C4
Ashbourne Rise	23 F2
Ashburn Ct	7 E3
Ashdale Rd	2 A3
Ashdown Clo	6 A5
Ashfield Clo	5 G3
Ashfield La	8 D2
Ashleigh Rd	4 C6
Ashley Gdns	23 G3
Ashmead Ct	7 G4
Ashmere Av	6 B5
Ashmore La	26 D2
Ashtree Clo	22 D2
Ashurst Clo	4 C4
Aspen Clo	24 A3
Aspen Copse	8 B5
Atkins Dri	20 B1
Atkinson Clo	23 H3
Audrey Clo	13 H3
Augustine Rd	10 C6
Augustus La	17 H6
Austin Av	16 A2
Austin Rd	18 A3
Avalon Clo	24 C1
Avalon Rd	24 C1
Avard Gdns	23 E2
Avebury Rd	23 F1
Avenue Rd	4 D4
Aviemore Clo	13 F2
Aviemore Way	13 F2
Avington Gro	4 D3
Avondale Rd, Bromley	6 D2
Avondale Rd, SE 9	2 C4
Axtaine Rd	18 D4
Aycliffe Clo	16 B1
Aylesbury Rd	7 E6
Aylesford Av	13 E2
Aylesham Rd	17 G4
Aynscombe Angle	18 A4
Babbacombe Rd	7 E4
Badgers Copse	17 G6
Bailey Pl	4 D2
Bakers Mews	23 G4
Balfour Rd	16 A2
Balgowan Rd	5 F6
Balmoral Av	13 F1
Banavie Gdns	6 A4
Bancroft Gdns	17 G5
Bankside Clo	30 C3
Bapchild Pl	18 B1
Barcombe Clo	9 H6
Barfield Rd	8 C6
Barfreston Way	4 C4
Bargrove Clo	4 B3
Barham Clo, Bromley Common	16 A5
Barham Clo, Chislehurst	8 D1
Barham Rd	8 C1
Bark Hart Rd	18 A5
Barnard Clo	9 F4
Barnesdale Cres	18 A3
Barnet Dri	14 A6
Barnet Wood Rd	15 G6
Barnfield Rd	10 C6
Barnfield Wood Clo	14 C3
Barnfield Wood Rd	14 B3
Barnhill Av	14 D2
Barnmead Rd	5 E4
Barry Clo	23 F1
Barson Clo	4 D3
Barwood Av	14 A5
Bassetts Clo	22 D2
Bassetts Way	22 D2
Baston Manor Rd	21 F2
Baston Rd	15 F5
Batchwood Grn	10 A6
Baths Rd	15 H1
Bay Tree Clo, Bromley	17 H2
Bay Tree Clo, St Mary Cray	18 B2
Beaconsfield Rd, Bromley	7 H6
Beaconsfield Rd, Mottingham	2 C4
Beadon Rd	15 E1
Beagles Clo	18 C6
Beamish Rd	18 C4
Beard Ter	5 G4
Beaumont Rd	17 E3
Beaver Clo	4 B3
Beaverwood Rd	9 G2
Bebletts Clo	23 H3
Beck Ct	4 D6
Beck La	5 E6
Beck River Park	5 G4
Beck Way	5 G6
Beckenham Gro	6 C5
Beckenham La	6 D5
Beckenham Place Pk	6 A3
Beckenham	5 E4
Beckenham Rd, West Wickham	14 A4
Beckett Walk	5 F1
Becketts Clo	23 G1
Beckford Dri	17 F4
Beddington Grn	9 G4
Beddington Path	9 G4
Beddington Rd	9 G4
Bedford Rd	18 A6
Beech Copse	8 B5
Beech Dell	22 B2
Beech Rd, Biggin Hill	30 C3
Beech Rd, Chelsfield	23 H5
Beechcroft	8 C3
Beechcroft Clo	23 F2
Beechcroft Rd	23 F2
Beeches Clo	4 D4
Beechfield Rd	7 G5
Beechmont Av	23 F4
Beechwood Dri	21 H2
Beechwood Rise	3 F6
Beeken Dri	22 D2
Belcroft Clo	7 E3
Belgrave Clo	18 C1
Bell Gdns	18 C2
Belle Vue Rd	27 H1
Bellefield Rd	18 A2
Belmont La	3 G6
Belmont Rd, Beckenham	5 F5
Belmont Rd, Chislehurst	8 D1
Belvedere Rd, Biggin Hill	31 F4
Belvedere Rd, SE 19	4 A3
Bencurtis Pk	20 C1
Benedict Clo	23 G2
Benenden Grn	15 E2
Bennetts Copse	8 A2
Berens Rd	18 C2
Berens Way	17 G1
Beresford Dri	8 A6
Berger Clo	17 F3
Berkeley Clo	17 F4
Berryfield Clo	8 A5
Berrylands	18 B6
Berrys Green Rd	31 H1
Berrys Hill	28 A6
Bertie Rd	5 E2
Berwick Way	17 H5
Bethersden Clo	5 G3
Betts Clo	5 F5
Betts Way	4 B3
Beverley Rd, Bromley	16 A6
Beverley Rd, SE 20	4 C6
Bevington Rd	5 H5
Bickley Cres	16 A1
Bickley Park Rd	8 B5
Bickley Rd	7 H5
Bicknor Rd	17 G4
Bidborough Clo	14 D2
Bilsby Gro	2 B6
Birch Av	16 C4
Birch Tree Av	20 D3
Birchington Clo	18 C5
Birchmead	5 G6
Birchwood Av	5 G6
Birchwood Rd	17 F1
Bird in Hand La	7 H5
Birdham Clo	16 A2
Birdhouse La	27 H6
Birkbeck Rd	4 D5
Birkdale Clo	17 H4
Bishop Butt Clo	23 G1
Bishops Gro	7 G6
Bishops Grn	7 G4
Bishops Walk	9 E4
Blackbrook La	16 B2
Blackness La	21 H6
Blacksmiths La	18 B2
Blackthorn Rd	31 E1
Blair Ct	5 H4
Blakeney Av	5 G4
Blakeney Rd	5 G3
Blanchard Clo	2 C5
Blandford Av	5 E5
Blandford Rd	4 D5
Blean Gro	4 D3
Blendon Path	6 D3
Blenheim Rd, Bromley	16 A1
Blenheim Rd, Orpington	18 B6
Blenheim Rd, SE 20	4 D3
Bloomfield Rd	15 H2
Bluebell Clo	16 D6
Blyth Rd	6 D4
Blythe Hill	9 H4
Bogey La	22 B6
Bolderwood Way	13 H6
Boleyn Gdns	14 A6
Boleyn Gro	14 A6
Bolton Clo	4 B5
Bolton Gdns	6 D2
Bombers La	32 C5
Bonar Pl	8 A3
Bonchester Clo	8 C4
Bonville Rd	7 E1
Border Cres	4 C1
Border Rd	4 C1
Borkwood Park	23 G2
Borkwood Way	23 F2
Bosco Clo	23 G2
Bostall Rd	10 A3
Boswell Clo	18 B4
Botany Bay La	8 D5
Boughton Av	15 E4
Boundary Clo	4 B5
Bourdon Rd	4 C5
Bourne Rd	15 H1
Bourne Vale	15 E5
Bourne Way	14 D6
Bournewood Rd	18 B4
Box Tree Walk	18 C5
Boyland Rd	6 D1
Brabourne Rise	14 B2
Bracken Hill Clo	6 D4
Bracken Hill La	6 D4
Brackenridge	6 D4
Brackley Rd	5 G3
Bradford Clo	16 B5
Braemar Gdns	14 A5
Braeside	5 H1
Bramerton Rd	5 F6
Bramley Clo	16 D5
Bramley Way	14 A6
Branston Cres	17 E5
Brantwood Way	10 B6
Brasted Clo	17 H6
Breakspears Dri	9 H4
Bredhurst Clo	4 D2
Brenchley Clo, Bromley	15 E3
Brenchley Clo, Chislehurst	8 C4
Brenchley Rd	16 A5
Brewery Rd	14 D5
Briar Gdns	20 A2
Briar La	20 A2
Briarswood Way	23 G3
Briary Gdns	7 F1
Brickfield Farm Gdns	22 D3
Bridgewater Clo	9 G6
Bridge Rd, Beckenham	5 F3
Bridge Rd, Orpington	18 A3
Bridgewood Clo	4 C3
Bridle Way	22 D2
Bridlington Clo	30 C4
Brimstone Clo	24 B5
Brindley Way	7 F1
Brittenden Clo	23 G4
Broad Oak Clo	9 H5
Broad Walk	24 C1
Broadcroft Rd	17 E4
Broadheath Dri	8 B1
Broadlands Rd	7 F1
Broadmeads Way	14 D2
Broadwater Gdns	22 D2
Brockwell Clo	17 H2
Brograve Gdns	6 A5
Broke Farm Dri	24 C6
Bromley Av	6 C3
Bromley Common	15 G…
Bromley Cres	6 D…
Bromley Gdns	6 D…
Bromley Gro	6 C
Bromley Hill	6 C
Bromley La	9 E
Bromley Rd, Beckenham	6 A
Bromley Rd, Bromley	6 C
Bromley Rd, Chislehurst	8 D
Brompton Clo	4 B
Brook La	7 E…
Brooklyn Rd	16 A
Brookmead Av	16 B
Brookmead Clo	18 A
Brookmead Way	18 A
Brooks Way	10 B
Brookside	17 G
Brookwood Clo	14 D
Broom Av	10 A
Broom Clo	16 A
Broomfield Rd	5 F…
Broomhill Rd	17 H…
Broomwood Rd	10 A
Broughton Rd	17 E
Brow Clo	18 C
Brow Cres	18 B…
Broxbourne Rd	17 G…
Bruce Gro	18 A…
Brunswick Pl	4 B…
Bruton Clo	8 B…
Buckhurst Rd	31 H…
Buckingham Clo	17 F…
Buckingham Dri	3 G…
Buckland Rd	23 G…
Bucks Cross Rd	24 D…
Budgins Hill	29 G…
Bull La	9 E…
Bullers Wood Dri	8 A…
Burford Rd	16 A…
Burham Clo	4 D…
Burlington Clo	16 D…
Burnham Way	5 F…
Burnhill Rd	5 F…
Burnt Ash La	7 E…
Burrell Row	5 G…
Burrfield Dri	18 C…
Burwood Av	15 F…
Bushell Way	8 C…
Bushey Av	17 F…
Bushey Way	14 B…
Buttermere Rd	18 C…
Bycroft St	5 E…
Byne Rd	4 D…
Byron Clo	4 C…
Cacketts La	28 C…
Cadogan Clo	6 C…
Cairndale Clo	6 D…
Calcott Walk	2 C…
Calverley Clo	5 H…
Calvin Clo	10 C…
Cambray Rd	17 H…
Cambridge Gro	4 C…
Cambridge Rd	7 E…
Camden Clo	8 D…
Camden Gro	8 D…
Camden Park Rd	8 B…
Camden Way	8 B…
Camelot Clo	30 D…
Cameron Rd	15 E…
Canbury Path	17 H…
Canon Rd	7 G…
Canterbury Clo	5 H…
Capel Clo	16 A…
Cardinal Clo	9 F…
Carisbrooke Rd	15 G…
Carlton Par	18 A…
Carlyle Av	7 H…
Carolyn Dri	24 A…
Carters Hill Clo	2 B…
Cascade Clo	10 C…
Castle Clo	6 C…
Castlecombe Rd	2 C…
Castledine Rd	4 C…
Castleton Rd	2 B…
Cathcart Dri	17 F…
Cator Rd	5 G…
Cator Rd	5 E…
Cattistock Rd	8 A…
Cavendish Way	13 H…
Caveside Clo	8 C…
Caygill Clo	14 D…
Cecil Way	15 F…

Foxgrove Rd 6 A3
Foxhome Clo 8 C2
Framlingham Cres 2 D6
Francis Rd 10 C6
Franklin Rd 4 D3
Frankswood Av 16 D2
Frant Clo 4 D3
Freelands Gro 7 F4
Freelands Rd 7 F4
Freesia Clo 23 G3
Freshwood Clo 5 H4
Friar Rd 18 A2
Frinsted Clo 18 C1
Fuller Clo 23 H3
Furzefield Clo 8 D2
Fyfe Way 7 E5
Fyfield Clo 14 C1

Gainsborough Clo 5 G3
Garden Cotts 10 C5
Garden La 7 F2
Garden Rd, Bromley 7 F3
Garden Rd, SE 20 4 D4
Garden Walk 5 G4
Gardiner Clo 10 C5
Garrard Clo 8 D1
Gates Green Rd 20 D1
Genoa Rd 4 C4
George Groves Rd 4 B4
George La 15 F5
Georges Clo 10 C6
Georgian Clo 15 F5
Giggs Hill 9 H5
Gilbert Rd 7 E3
Gillmans Rd 18 B5
Gilroy Way 18 B4
Glades Pl 7 E5
Gladstone Mews 4 D3
Gladstone Rd 23 E3
Gladwell Rd 7 F2
Glanfield Rd 13 G1
Glanville Rd 7 F6
Glassmill La 7 E5
Glebe House Dri 15 F5
Glebe Rd 7 E4
Glebe Way 14 B6
Gleeson Dri 23 G3
Glendale Mews 6 A4
Glendower Cres 18 A3
Gleneagles Clo 17 F5
Gleneagles Grn 17 F5
Glentrammon Av 23 G4
Glentrammon Clo 23 H4
Glentrammon Gdns 23 G4
Glentrammon Rd 23 G4
Glenview Rd 7 H5
Gload Cres 18 C6
Glyndebourne Pk 16 D6
Goddard Rd 13 E1
Goddington Chase 24 A2
Goddington La 23 H1
Godwin Rd 7 G6
Goldfinch Clo 24 A3
Golf Rd 8 C6
Goodhart Way 14 C4
Goodmead Rd 18 A4
Goose Green Clo 10 A5
Gordon Rd, Beckenham 5 F6
Gordon Rd, Elmers End 5 E5
Gordon Way 7 E4
Gorse Rd 25 F1
Gosshill Rd 8 C5
Gossington Clo 3 F6
Gowland Pl 5 F5
Grampian Clo 17 G3
Grand View Av 30 C2
Grange Dri, Chislehurst 8 A2
Grange Dri, Pratts Bottom 24 B6
Grange Rd 17 E6
Grangewood La 5 G2
Grasmere Av 22 C1
Grasmere Gdns 22 D1
Grasmere Rd, Bromley 6 D4
Grasmere Rd, Orpington 22 C1
Gravel Pit Way 17 H6
Gravel Rd 16 A6
Gravelwood Clo 3 G5
Graveney Gro 4 D3
Grayland Clo 7 H4
Grays Farm Rd 10 B4
Grays Rd 31 H6
Great Elms Rd 15 G1
Great Thrift 17 E1
Greatwood 8 C3
Green Clo 6 C6
Green Farm Clo 23 G4
Green Gdns 23 E3
Green Hill 27 G3
Green La, Chislehurst 8 D1
Green La, SE 20 5 E3
Green Way 16 A3
Greenacres Clo 22 D2
Greencourt Rd, Crockenhill 19 H2
Greencourt Rd, Petts Wood 17 F2
Greenfield Gdns 17 E4
Greenleigh Av 18 A1
Greenoak Rise 30 D3
Greenside Walk 30 C4
Greenway 8 C1
Greenways 5 H5
Greenwood Clo 17 F3
Gresham Rd 5 E5
Greycot Rd 5 H1
Greys Park Clo 21 G3
Grice Av 26 D4
Grosvenor Rd, Petts Wood 17 G3
Grosvenor Rd, West Wickham 14 A5
Grove Clo 15 E6
Grove Park Rd 2 B5
Grove Vale 8 E2
Groveland Rd 5 F6
Grovelands Rd 10 A3
Gumping Rd 17 E5
Gundulph Rd 7 G6
Gwydor Rd 5 E6
Gwydyr Rd 7 E6

Hackington Cres 5 H2
Haddon Rd 18 C2
Hadlow Pl 4 B3
Haig Rd 31 E2
Haileybury Rd 24 A2
Hale Clo 23 E2
Hall View 2 B4
Hallam Clo 8 B1
Hambro Av 15 E5
Hamlet Rd 4 A3
Hammelton Rd 7 E4
Hampden Av 5 F5
Hampden Rd 5 F3
Hanbury Dri 26 D4
Hangrove Hill 28 A4
Hannah Clo 6 A6
Hanover Dri 3 G6
Hanson Clo 5 H3
Harbledown Pl 18 B1
Hardcourts Clo 20 A1
Hardings La 5 E2
Harlands Gro 22 D2
Harley Gdns 23 F2
Harleyford 7 G4
Harrow Gdns 24 A2
Hart Dyke Rd 18 C5
Hartfield Cres 21 E1
Hartfield Gro 4 C4
Hartfield Rd 21 E2
Harting Rd 2 C5
Hartley Clo 8 B5
Harton Clo 7 H4
Harvel Clo 9 H6
Harvest Bank Rd 21 E1
Harwood Av 7 F5
Hassock Wood 21 H2
Hassop Walk 2 C5
Hastings Rd 16 A5
Hathaway Clo 16 B5
Havelock Rd 15 G1
Haven Clo 2 D5
Haverthwaite Rd 17 F6
Hawes La 14 B5
Hawes Rd 7 F4
Hawfield Bank 24 C1
Hawkeshead Clo 6 D3
Hawkhurst Way 14 A6
Hawkinge Walk 10 B6
Hawksbrook La 14 A3
Hawkwood La 9 E4
Hawstead La 25 E3
Hawthorn Clo 17 F3
Hawthorn Dri 20 D2
Hawthorn Gro 4 C4
Hawthorndene Clo 15 E6
Hawthorndene Rd 15 E6
Hawthorne Av 31 E1
Hawthorne Clo 8 B6
Hawthorne Rd 8 A6
Haxted Rd 7 F4
Haydens Clo 18 B3
Hayes Chase 14 C3
Hayes Clo 15 E6
Hayes Gdn 15 E6
Hayes Hill 14 C5
Hayes Hill Rd 14 D5
Hayes La, Beckenham 6 A6
Hayes La, Bromley 15 F2
Hayes Mead Rd 14 D5
Hayes Rd 15 E1
Hayes St 15 F5
Hayes Way 14 A1
Hayes Wood Av 15 F5
Hayesford Park Dri 15 E2
Hayfield Rd 18 A2
Hayne Rd 5 G5
Haysleigh Gdns 4 B5
Haywood Rise 23 G3
Haywood Road 15 H1
Hazel Gro 16 C6
Hazel Walk 16 C3
Hazelhurst 6 B4
Hazelmere Rd 17 E1
Hazelmere Way 15 E3
Hazelwood Rd 28 C3
Headcorn Rd 7 E1
Healy Dri 23 H1
Hearns Clo 18 B1
Hearns Rise 18 C1
Hearns Road 18 B1
Heath Clo 18 B3
Heath Gro 4 D3
Heath Park Dri 8 A6
Heath Rise 15 E3
Heath Side 17 E4
Heatherbank 8 C5
Heathfield 9 E2
Heathfield Clo 21 G3
Heathfield La 8 D2
Heathfield Rd, Bromley 6 D3
Heathfield Rd, Keston 21 G3
Heathley End 9 E2
Henderson Rd 26 D3
Hengist Way 14 C1
Henry St 7 F4
Henson Clo 16 D6
Henville Rd 7 G4
Hepburn Gdns 14 D5
Herbert Rd 16 A2
Heritage Hill 21 G3
Heron Court 15 G1
Hever Gdns 8 C5
Hewitts Rd 25 E5
High Beeches 24 A4
High Broom Cres 14 A4
High Elms Rd 22 D6
High Grove 7 G4
High Mead 14 C6
High St, Beckenham 5 G5
High St, Bromley 7 E5
High St, Chislehurst 8 D2
High St, Downe 27 H2
High St, Farnborough 22 D3
High St, Green Street Green 23 G4
High St, Orpington 17 H5
High St, St Mary Cray 18 B3
High St, SE 20 4 C2
High St, West Wickham 14 A5
High Tor Clo 7 F3
High View Rd 27 H1
Highams Hill 26 B3
Highbury Clo 14 A6
Highcombe Clo 2 C3
Highfield Av 23 H3
Highfield Dri, Bromley 14 D1
Highfield Dri, West Wickham 20 A1
Highfield Rd, Biggin Hill 30 C2
Highfield Rd, Bromley 16 B1
Highfield Rd, St Pauls Cray 9 G6
Highgrove Clo 8 A4
Highgrove Ct 5 G3
Highland Croft 5 H2
Highland Rd 6 D4
Highlands Rd 18 B4
Highview 8 B3
Highwood Clo 17 E6
Highwood Dri 16 D6
Hilborough Way 23 F3
Hilda Vale Clo 22 C2
Hilda Vale Rd 22 C2
Hildenlea Pl 6 C5
Hill Brow 7 H4
Hill Clo 8 C1
Hill Crest Rd 30 D1
Hill End 17 H6
Hillbrow Rd 6 C3
Hillcrest Clo 13 F3
Hillcrest Rd, Bromley 7 E1
Hillcrest Rd, Orpington 18 A6
Hillcrest View 13 F3
Hilldown Rd 14 D5
Hilldrop Rd 7 F2
Hillingdale 30 C3
Hillside La 14 D6
Hillside Rd 6 D6
Hilltop Gdns 17 F6
Hillview Cres 17 G5
Hillview Rd, Chislehurst 8 C1
Hillview Rd, Orpington 17 G5
Hoblands End 9 G2
Hockenden La 11 F6
Hodsoll Ct 18 C2
Hodson Cres 18 C2
Hogtrough Hill 32 D5
Holbrook La 9 F3
Holbrook Way 16 B3
Holland Clo 14 D6
Holland Way 14 D6
Holligrave Rd 7 E4
Hollingworth Rd 16 D4
Holly Cres 13 G2
Holly Rd 23 H5
Hollybrake Clo 9 E3
Hollybush La 25 F4
Hollydale Dri 22 B1
Holmbury Pk 8 A3
Holmcroft Way 16 B2
Holmdale Rd 8 D1
Holmdene Clo 6 A5
Holwood Park Av 22 B2
Home Lea 23 G3
Homefield Clo 18 B1
Homefield Mews 5 G4
Homefield Rise 17 H5
Homefield Road 7 G4
Homemead Rd 16 B2
Homesdale Rd, Bromley 7 G6
Homesdale Rd, Orpington 17 F4
Homestead Rd 24 A5
Homewood Cres 9 F3
Honeybourne Way 17 E5
Hood Av 18 A2
Hook Farm Rd 15 G2
Hookwood Rd 29 H2
Hope Park 6 D3
Horley Rd 2 C5
Hornbeam Way 16 C3
Horning Clo 2 D5
Horsecroft Clo 18 A5
Horsell Rd 10 A4
Horsley Rd 7 F4
Horsmonden Clo 17 G4
Howard Rd, Bromley 7 E3
Howard Rd, SE 20 4 D4
Howards Crest Clo 6 B5
Hunters Gro 22 D2
Hunts Mead Clo 8 B4
Hurst Clo 14 D5
Hurstdene Av 14 D5
Hurstfield 15 E2
Hurstwood Dri 8 B6
Husseywell Cres 15 E5
Hyde Dri 18 A1
Hythe Clo 18 B1

Ickleton Rd 2 D6
Iden Clo 6 C6
Imperial Way 3 G5
Inchwood 20 A2
INDUSTRIAL ESTATES:
Airport Ind Est 27 E6
Beckenham Bus. Centre 5 F2
Biggin Hill Bus. Park 27 E6
Broomsleigh Bus. Park 5 G1
Concorde Bus. Park 27 E6
Crayfield Ind Park 10 C5
Franklin Ind Est 4 D4
Kangley Bus. Centre 5 F1
Metro Bus. Centre 5 G1
Murray Bus. Centre 10 B6
Nugent Ind Park 18 B2
Orchard Bus. Centre 5 F1
Ravensquay Bus. Centre 18 B2
Station Estate 13 E1
Ingleby Way 8 C1
Ingleside Clo 5 G3
Inglewood Copse 8 A5
Invicta Clo 8 C1
Irene Rd 17 H4
Irvine Way 17 G4
Isabella Dri 22 D2
Islehurst Clo 8 C4
Ivychurch Clo 4 C3

Jackass La 21 F4
Jackson Rd 16 A6
Jaffray Rd 15 H1
Jail La 31 F1
Jasmine Clo 16 C6
Jasmine Gro 4 C4
Jersey Dri 17 E3
Jevington Way 2 A3
Jewels Hill 26 B4
Johnson Rd 15 H2
Jubilee Rd 25 F4
Jug Hill 30 D1
Juglans Rd 17 H5
Julian Rd 24 A4
Juniper Clo 31 F2

Kangley Bridge Rd 5 G1
Karen Ct 6 D4
Kechill Gdns 15 E4
Kedleston Dri 17 G3
Keedonwood Rd 6 C1
Keith Park Cres 26 D4
Kelsey La 5 G6
Kelsey Park Av 6 A5
Kelsey Park Rd 5 H5
Kelsey Rd 10 B5
Kelsey Sq 5 G5
Kelsey Way 5 G6
Kelvin Par 17 F5
Kemble Dri 22 A1
Kembleside Rd 30 C3
Kemerton Rd 6 A5
Kemnal Rd 9 E3
Kemsing Clo 15 E6
Kendall Av 5 F5
Kendall Rd 5 F5
Kenilworth Rd, Petts Wood 17 E3
Kenilworth Rd, SE 20 5 E4
Kenley Clo 9 G6
Kennedy Clo 17 E5
Kent Clo 23 G4
Kent House La 5 F2
Kent House Rd 5 E4
Kent Rd, Orpington 18 B3
Kent Rd, West Wickham 14 A5
Kentish Way 7 E5
Kenwood Dri 6 A6
Kersey Gdns 2 C6
Keston Av 21 G3
Keston Gdns 21 G2
Keston Park Clo 22 B1
Keswick Rd, Orpington 17 H5
Keswick Rd, West Wickham 14 C6
Kevington Clo 17 H1
Kevington Dri 17 G1
Keymer Clo 30 D1
Killewarren Way 18 B4
Kimberley Gate 6 D3
Kimberley Rd 5 E5
Kimmeridge Gdns 2 C6
Kimmeridge Rd 2 C6
King George VI Av 31 E2
King Henrys Dri 26 A2
King Henrys Mews 23 G3
King Johns Walk 2 B3
King and Queen Clo 2 D6
Kingfisher Clo 18 C1
Kingfisher Way 13 E2
Kings Av 6 D2
Kings Hall Rd 5 E3
Kings Rd, Biggin Hill 30 D1
Kings Rd, Orpington 23 G2
Kingsdale Rd 5 E4
Kingsdown Way 15 E3
Kingsgate Clo 10 B6
Kingsleigh Walk 14 D1
Kingsley Mews 8 D2
Kingsley Rd 23 G5
Kingsmead 31 E1
Kingston Cres 5 G4
Kingsway, Petts Wood 17 E2
Kingsway, West Wickham 20 D1
Kingswood Av 14 C1
Kingswood Clo 17 F4
Kingswood Rd, Shortlands 6 C6
Kingswood Rd, SE 20 4 D2
Kingsworth Clo 13 F2
Kinnaird Av 6 D2
Kinnaird Clo 6 D2
Kippington Dri 2 C3
Kirkstone Way 6 D3
Knights Ridge 24 B3
Knoll Rise 17 G5
Knowle Rd 16 A6
Knowlton Grn 15 E2
Koonowla Clo 31 E1
Kydbrook Clo 17 E4
Kynaston Rd, Bromley 7 E1
Kynaston Rd, Orpington 18 B4

La Tourne Gdns 23 E1
Laburnum Way 16 C4
Ladycroft Gdns 23 E3
Ladycroft Way 22 D3
Ladywood Av 17 G2

agoon Rd	18 B2	Long Acre	18 C6
ake Av	7 E2	Long Meadow Clo	14 B4
akes Rd	21 G3	Longbury Clo	10 A6
akeside	6 A6	Longbury Dri	10 A6
akeside Dri	22 A1	Longdon Wood	22 A2
akeswood Rd	16 D3	Longfield	7 E4
ambardes Clo	29 G2	Longleat Mews	18 B1
amberhurst Clo	18 C5	Longmead	8 C5
ambert Clo	30 D1	Loop Rd	8 D2
ambscroft Av	2 B5	Lotus Rd	31 F3
amorna Clo	17 H4	Love La	4 C6
ancaster Clo	14 D1	Lovelace Av	16 C3
ancing Rd	18 A6	Lovibonds Av	22 D2
andsdowne Av	16 D5	Lower Camden	8 B3
andsdowne Rd	7 F3	Lower Gravel Rd	16 A5
aneside	8 D1	Lower Rd	18 B3
angdale Clo	22 D1	Loxwood Clo	18 C6
angdon Rd	7 F6	Lubbock Rd	8 B3
angley Gdns, Hayes	15 G1	Lucas Rd	4 D2
angley Gdns, Southborough	16 D3	Lucerne Rd	17 H5
angley Rd	13 E1	Ludlow Clo	7 E6
angley Way	14 C5	Lullarook Clo	30 C2
ankton Rd	6 A4	Lullingstone Clo	10 A3
apworth Clo	18 B6	Lullingstone Cres	10 A3
arch Dene	16 C6	Lullington Garth	6 D3
arch Way	16 C4	Lullington Rd	4 B3
arkfield Clo	15 E6	Lulworth Rd	6 C4
arkspur Clo	18 B6	Lunar Clo	31 E1
atham Clo	30 C2	Lusted Hall La	30 C5
aurel Gro	4 C3	Luxted Rd	27 H3
awn Clo	7 F3	Lychgate Rd	18 A5
awn Rd	5 G3	Lyndhurst Clo	22 D2
awrie Park Cres	4 C1	Lynmouth Rise	18 A1
awrie Park Rd	4 C2	Lynne Clo	23 G4
axey Rd	23 G4	Lynstead Ct	5 F5
ayhams Rd	20 C2	Lynsted Clo	7 G5
ayzell Walk	2 C3	Lynton Av	18 A1
ea Rd	5 H5	Lynwood Gro	17 G4
eafy Gro	21 G3	Lyoth Rd	17 E6
eamington Av, Bromley	7 G1	Lysander Way	23 E1
eamington Av, Orpington	23 F2	Lytchet Rd	7 F3
eamington Clo	7 G1		
eas Grn	13 H1	Maberley Cres	4 B3
eaveland Clo	13 H1	Maberley Rd, Beckenham	5 E6
eaves Green Cres	27 E2	Maberley Rd, SE 19	4 B4
eaves Green Rd	21 H6	Mace La	28 B5
ebanon Gdns	31 E2	Mackenzie Rd	4 D5
edrington Rd	4 A2	Madeline Rd	22 D1
eeds Clo	18 C6	Madeira Av	4 B4
eesons Hill	9 G6	Madison Gdns	6 C3
eesons Way	9 G5	Magdalen Gro	24 A2
eith Hill	9 H4	Magnolia Dri	31 E1
eith Hill Grn	9 H4	Magpie Hall Clo	16 A4
ennard Av	14 D6	Magpie Hall La	16 A4
ennard Clo	14 D6	Main Rd, Biggin Hill	30 D1
ennard Rd, Beckenham	4 D2	Main Rd, St Pauls Cray	10 B4
ennard Rd, Bromley	16 B5	Mainridge Rd	3 E6
etchworth Clo	15 E2	Maitland Rd	5 E2
etchworth Dri	15 E2	Malan Clo	31 E2
ewes Rd	7 H5	Malcolm Rd	4 D3
eybourne Clo	15 E3	Mallard Walk	13 E2
ezayre Rd	23 G4	Malling Way	14 D4
ichlade Clo	23 G2	Malmains Clo	14 B1
iddon Rd	7 G6	Malmains Way	14 B1
illie Rd	30 D3	Maltby Clo	17 H5
ime Clo	16 A1	Malvern Clo	4 B5
ime Gro	16 D6	Malvern Rd	24 A2
ime Tree Walk	20 D2	Manning Rd	18 C2
imes Av	4 C3	Manor Park	9 E5
imes Rd	6 A5	Manor Park Clo	14 A5
imes Row	22 D3	Manor Park Rd, Chislehurst	9 E4
incoln Green Rd	17 H2	Manor Park Rd, West Wickham	14 A5
inden Clo	23 H3	Manor Pl	9 E5
inden Gro	4 D2	Manor Rd, Beckenham	5 H5
inden Leas	14 B6	Manor Way, West Wickham	13 H6
indenfield	8 D5	Manor View	5 G5
indsey Clo	7 H6	Manor Way, Beckenham	5 H5
ink Way	16 A4	Manor Way, Bromley	16 A3
inkfield	15 E3	Manor Way, Petts Wood	17 E2
inks Rd	14 B5	Manorfields Clo	9 G6
inks Way	13 H3	Mansfield Clo	18 C4
inslade Rd	23 H4	Manston Clo	4 D4
iskeard Clo	9 E2	Maple Clo	17 F2
ittle Acre	5 H6	Maple Leaf Clo	31 E2
ittle Court	14 C6	Maple Rd	4 C4
ittle Redlands	8 A5	Mapledene	9 E1
ittle Thrift	16 D1	Mapleton Clo	15 E2
ittlejohn Rd	18 A3	Marcellina Way	23 G1
ittlestone Clo	5 H2	Marden Av	15 E3
loyds Way	13 F2	Marina Clo	17 E6
ockesley Dri	17 H3	Marion Cres	18 A2
odge Av	18 A5	Marke Clo	22 A2
odge Cres	18 A5	Market Meadow & William Pl	18 B1
odge Gdns	13 G2		
ogs Hill	7 G3		
ogs Hill Clo	8 A4		
ondon La	6 D3		
ondon Rd	6 D3		

Market Sq	7 E5	Morris Clo, Farnborough	23 F1
Markwell Clo	14 D6	Morris Clo, Upper Elmers End	13 E3
Marlborough Clo	17 G4	Morston Gdns	2 D6
Marlborough Rd	15 G1	Mortimer Rd, Biggin Hill	26 D3
Marlings Clo	17 G1	Mortimer Rd, Orpington	18 A5
Marlings Park Av	17 G1	Moselle Rd	31 F3
Marlow Clo	4 C6	Mosslea Rd, Bromley	15 H2
Marlow Rd	4 C6	Mosslea Rd, Orpington	22 D1
Marlowe Clo	9 E3	Mosslea Rd, SE 20	4 D3
Marsden Way	23 G2	Mosul Way	16 A3
Marsham Clo	8 C1	Mosyer Rd	18 C6
Martindale Av	23 H3	Mottingham Gdns	2 C3
Martins Clo, St Pauls Cray	10 C6	Mottingham Rd	2 A3
Martins Clo, West Wickham	14 C6	Mottingham Rd	2 C4
Martins Rd	6 D5	Mouchotte Clo	26 D3
Masefield View	22 D1	Mount Clo	8 A4
Masons Hill	7 F6	Mount Av	14 C6
Matfield Clo	15 E2	Mount Court	30 D2
Mavelstone Clo	8 A4	Mount Pleasant	18 B1
Mavelstone Rd	7 H4	Mountfield Way	14 D4
Mavelstone Rd	23 G1	Mounthurst Rd	17 H4
Maxwell Gdns	18 A2	Mountview Rd	16 C6
May Av	4 C2	Mummery Way	18 C4
Maybourne Clo	16 D2	Mungo Park Way	7 F5
Maybury Clo	5 H4	Murray Av	10 B6
Mayfare Clo	17 G5	Murray Rd	
Mayfield Av	16 A2		
Mayfield Rd	5 E6	Napier Rd	15 F1
Mayford Clo	25 E3	Narrow Way	16 A3
Maypole Rd	6 C5	Nash Grn	7 E2
Mays Hill Rd	5 H3	Nash La	21 E5
Maywood Clo	8 D2	Nelson Clo	31 E2
Mead Rd	14 D3	Nelson Rd	15 G1
Mead Way	8 D1	Nettlestead Clo	5 G4
Meadow Clo	6 D5	New Barn La	28 B6
Meadow Rd	15 G1	New Farm Av	15 E1
Meadow View	10 B6	New Mill Rd	10 B4
Meadow Way	22 C1	New Rd	17 H4
Meadowcroft	8 B6	New Road Hill	22 B6
Meadway	6 B4	New Street Hill	7 F1
Meaford Way	18 A2	Newbury Rd	7 E6
Melanda Clo	8 B1	Newing Green	7 H3
Melbourne Clo, Orpington	17 G4	Newlands Park	4 D2
Melbourne Clo, Penge	4 B3	Newman Rd	7 F4
Meldrum Clo	18 C3	Newnhams Clo	8 B6
Melis Cres	4 B4	Newstead Av	17 F6
Melody Rd	30 C4	Nichol La	7 F3
Melrose Cres	23 F3	Nicolson Rd	18 C4
Melrose Rd	30 D1	Nightingale La	7 G5
Melvin Rd	4 D4	Nightingale Rd	16 D3
Mere Clo	16 C6	Ninhams Wood	22 C2
Mere Side	16 C6	Norheads La	30 A4
Merewood Clo	8 C5	Norlands Cres	8 D5
Mereworth Clo	14 D2	Norlands Gate	8 D4
Meriden Clo	7 H4	Norman Clo	23 E1
Merlewood Dri	13 G1	Normanhurst Rd	10 B5
Merlin Gro	5 E2	Norsted La	29 G2
Merrydown Way	30 D2	North Dri	23 G2
Merryhills Clo	4 C4	North End La	22 C6
Mersham Pl	4 C4	North Pole La	21 E4
Mertton Gdns	16 D2	North Rd, Bromley	7 F4
Mewsend	30 D3	North Rd, West Wickham	14 A5
Mickleham Clo	9 H5	North St	7 E4
Mickleham Rd	9 H4	Northbourne	15 E4
Midfield Way	9 H4	Northfield Clo	18 B3
Milestone Rd	4 A2	Northfield Clo	8 A4
Milk St	7 F2	Northlands Av	23 F2
Milking La	27 E3	Northolme Rise	17 G6
Mill Brook Rd	18 B1	Northside Rd	7 E4
Mill La	27 H1	Northumberland Gdns	16 C1
Mill Pl	8 C4	Novar Clo	17 H4
Mill Vale	7 E5	Nunnington Clo	2 C5
Millfields Clo	18 B1	Nursery Clo	17 H4
Millwood Rd	10 C6	Nursery Gdns	8 D2
Mimosa Clo	18 B6	Nut Tree Clo	24 D1
Minden Rd	4 C4	Nutfield Way	16 C6
Ministry Way	2 D4		
Minshull Pl	5 H3	Oak Gro	14 B6
Minster Rd	7 F3	Oak Lodge Dri	14 A4
Mitchell Clo	23 G2	Oak Rd	23 H5
Mitchell Rd	7 E4	Oak Tree Gdns	7 F1
Moat Clo	23 H5	Oakbrook Clo	7 F1
Model Farm Clo	2 C4	Oakdene Av	8 B1
Molash Rd	18 C1	Oakdene Rd	17 H3
Monarch Clo	21 E2	Oakfield Gdns	13 H2
Monivea Rd	5 G3	Oakfield La	21 G2
Monk Way	13 H3	Oakfield Rd, Orpington	18 A4
Monks Way	17 E5	Oakfield Rd, SE 20	4 D5
Mons Way	16 A3	Oakgrove Rd	15 E1
Montcalm Clo	15 E3	Oakham Dri	16 A2
Montrave Rd	4 D3	Oakhill Rd, Beckenham	4 C4
Moorcroft Gdns	16 A2	Oakhill Rd, Orpington	17 G5
Mooreland Rd	7 E3	Oaklands Av	5 E3
Moorfield Rd	18 A4	Oaklands La	30 C1
Morgan Rd	7 E3	Oaklands Rd	6 D3
Morland Rd	5 E3	Oakleigh Gdns	23 G2
Morley Clo	16 D6		
Morley Rd	9 E4		
Mornington Av	7 G6		
Mornington Clo	30 D2		

Oakleigh Park Av	8 C4	Packham Clo	18 B6
Oakley Dri	22 A1	Paddock Clo	22 D2
Oakley Rd	16 A6	Paddock Way	9 F3
Oakmead Av	15 E3	Paddocks Clo	18 C6
Oakmont Pl	17 F5	Padua Rd	4 D4
Oakway	6 B5	Page Heath La	7 H6
Oakwood Av, Beckenham	6 A5	Page Heath Villas	7 H6
Oakwood Av, Bromley	7 F6	Paget Gdns	8 D4
Oakwood Clo	8 B2	Palace Gro, Bromley	7 F4
Oakwood Gdns	17 E6	Palace Gro, SE 19	4 A3
Oakwood Rd	17 E6	Palace Rd, Bromley	7 F4
Oasthouse Way	18 B1	Palace Rd, SE 19	4 A3
Oates Clo	6 B6	Palace Sq	4 A3
Oatfield Rd	17 H5	Palace View	7 F6
Ockham Dri	10 A3	Palewell Clo	10 A5
Offenham Rd	2 D6	Pallant Way	22 C1
Okemore Gdns	18 B1	Palmarsh Clo	18 C1
Old Harrow La	32 A4	Palmer Ct	20 B1
Old Hill, Chislehurst	8 C4	Palmerston Rd	23 E3
Old Hill, Green Street Green	23 F4	Parish La	5 E3
Old Homesdale Rd	15 G1	Parish Mews	5 E3
Old London Rd	24 D6	Park Av, Bromley	6 D3
Old Maidstone Rd	11 E3	Park Av, Farnborough	16 B6
Old Manor Way	8 B1	Park Av, Orpington	17 H6
Old Perry St	9 F3	Park Av, West Wickham	14 A6
Old School Clo	5 E5	Park End	6 D4
Old Tye Av	31 E1	Park Farm Clo	7 H4
Oldbury Clo	18 C1	Park Gro	7 F4
Oldfield Clo	16 B1	Park Hill	16 A1
Oldfield Grange	16 B1	Park Hill Rd	6 C5
Oldfield Rd	16 A1	Park Mews	8 D2
Oleander Clo	23 F3	Park Rd, Beckenham	5 G3
Olyffe Dri	6 A4	Park Rd, Bromley	7 F4
Onslow Cres	8 D4	Park Rd, Chislehurst	8 D2
Orange Court La	22 C6		
Orchard Grn	17 G6		
Orchard Gro, Orpington	17 H6		
Orchard Gro, Penge	4 B3		
Orchard Rd, Bromley	7 G4		
Orchard Rd, Farnborough	22 D3		
Orchard Rd, Pratts Bottom	24 B6		
Oregon Sq	17 F5		
Orlestone Gdns	24 D3		
Ormonde Av	16 D6		
Orpington Rd	17 G1		
Orpington-by-Pass	24 B2		
Osborne Rd	13 F1		
Osgood Av	23 G3		
Osgood Gdns	23 G3		
Ospringe Clo	4 D4		
Osterley Clo	9 H4		
Otford Clo, Bickley	8 C6		
Otford Clo, Penge	4 D4		
Otlinge Clo	18 D1		
Ottenden Clo	23 G2		
Overbrae	5 H2		
Overbury Av	6 A6		
Overhill Way	14 B2		
Overstand Clo	13 H2		
Owen Walk (FP)	4 B4		
Oxenden Wood Rd	24 B4		
Oxhawth Cres	16 C2		